Celebrate!

Christmas

Mike Hirst

WAYLAND

CHINESE NEW YEAR

DIWALI

ID-UL-FITR

**All Wayland books encourage children
to read and help them improve their literacy.**

- ✓ The contents page, page numbers, headings and index help locate specific pieces of information.

- ✓ The glossary reinforces alphabetic knowledge and extends vocabulary.

- ✓ The 'finding out more' section suggests other books dealing with the same subject.

find Wayland on the Internet at http://www.wayland.co.uk

This book is based on the original title **Christmas** in the *Festivals* series, published in 1996 by Wayland Publishers Ltd.

Editor: Philippa Smith
Designers: Tim Mayer and Malcolm Walker

First published in 1999 by Wayland Publishers Ltd,
61 Western Road, Hove, East Sussex BN3 1JD

British Library Cataloguing in Publication Data
Hirst, Mike
   Christmas. – (Celebrate!)
   1. Christmas – Juvenile literature
   I. Title
   263.9'15

ISBN 0 7502 2527 0

Printed and bound by Eurografica S.p.A., Italy

Cover picture: Christmas time in Sydney, Australia, is in the summer when the weather is hot and sunny.

Picture acknowledgments
Associated Press/Topham/J Bouju 26 (top); Cephas:
J. Riviere 20; Mary Evans Picture Library: 8, 9, 10, 11, 12 (both); Eye Ubiquitous: Laurence Fordyce 29; Sally and Richard Greenhill: 19; Christine Osborne: 4, 18 (top), 23, 26 (bottom), 28; Panos: *cover* Penny Tweedie; Topham Picturepoint: 13, 14, 15, 17 (top), 18 (bottom), 22, 24; Trip: C. Caffrey 5, 6, A. Tjagny 4, 7, 17, (bottom), V. Kolpakov 17 (top), A. Tjagny 21, I. Souriment 5, 25, A.Tjagny-Rjadno 27; Wayland Picture Library: Paul Seheult 25 (top) and title page, Tim Woodcock 29 (bottom).
Border and cover artwork by Tim Mayer.

Contents

Words that appear in **bold** in the text
are explained in the glossary on page 30.

Christmas Around the World

◄ In Russia, Christians celebrate Christmas on 6 January.

▲ In Germany, boys dress up as the wise men and sing **carols**.

▲ A church service at Bethlehem, in Israel, the place where Jesus was born.

▲ In Goa, India, Christians remember the three wise men on 6 January.

▲ Christmas trees and poinsettia plants decorate a church in New York city.

▲ A family in Korea open their presents beside their Christmas tree.

▼ Statues form part of a **nativity** scene outside a church in Mexico.

◄ In Australia, Christmas is in the middle of summer, so Christmas lunch is a picnic outside.

Merry Christmas

The first Christmas

Jesus was born about 2,000 years ago. His parents were called Joseph and Mary.

Joseph and Mary had to go to a town called Bethlehem. It was very busy there, and they could not find a place to stay. They had to sleep in a stable overnight with the cows and donkeys.

During the night, Jesus was born.

What do you think about if you hear the word 'Christmas'? Is it an exciting time for you?

Maybe you think about presents or Father Christmas. Some people have a Christmas tree and a party. Do you think about the baby Jesus, shepherds and wise men?

In many countries, Christmas is a holiday time. People stop going to work or school, and visit their friends and families.

For Christians, Christmas is a time to think about the birth of Jesus.

► These statues tell the story of how Jesus was born. Baby Jesus was visited by three wise men.

◄ Christians go to special church services at Christmas. Most Christians celebrate Christmas on 25 December.

Christians believe that Jesus was the son of God. He came to earth to show them how to be good people. Jesus also showed people how much God loves them. Christians want everyone to be happy at Christmas, and show kindness to other people.

Winter Festivals

In the northern parts of the world, Christmas happens in the middle of winter.

Even before Jesus was born, people had winter festivals. At this time of year, the weather is cold, and the sun is at its weakest.

◄ The Romans had a winter festival that lasted for ten days. Their slaves had a holiday and could do whatever they liked.

In northern Europe, people had a festival called Yule. They lit big fires and said prayers to the sun, asking it to come back again in the spring. They needed sunshine to grow their crops.

In Italy, the Romans also had a winter holiday, called Saturnalia. They worshipped the god Saturn with parties and feasting. Saturn was the Roman god of the harvest.

The Lord of Misrule

In the **Middle Ages**, townspeople in Europe had many parties, games and feasts at Christmas time. A man called the Lord of Misrule was in charge of the festival.

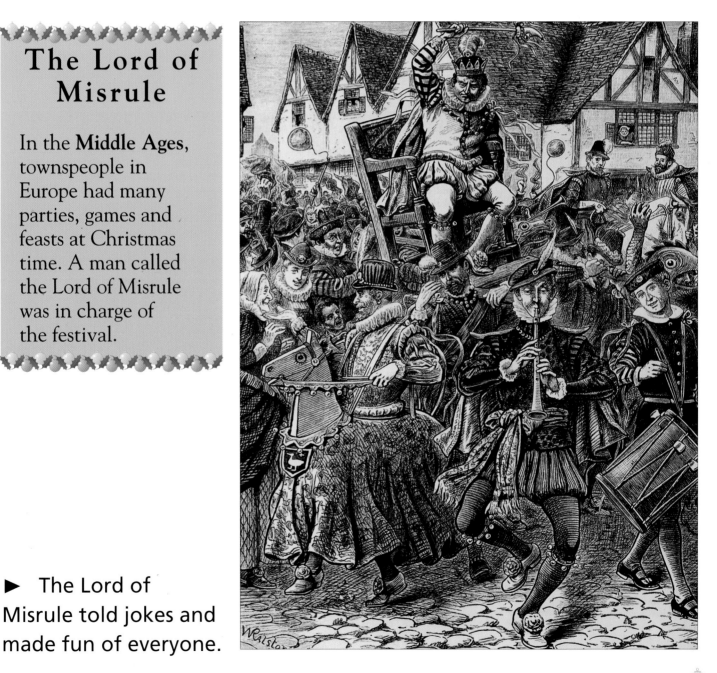

► The Lord of Misrule told jokes and made fun of everyone.

► This picture from an old book shows children dragging a Yule log home.

Yule Log

At the winter festival of Yule, people cut a huge log of wood. They put green leaves and ribbons on the log, and then set it on fire.

The log burned for days and days. People believed it had the magic power to make the sun come back in the spring.

After Jesus was born, more and more people in Europe became Christians. They wanted a winter festival to celebrate the birthday of Jesus.

The first Christians began to celebrate Christmas at the same time as the festivals of Yule and Saturnalia.

An important Christian leader was the **Pope** in Rome. He decided that people should remember the birth of Jesus on 25 December. This was how Christmas Day came to be on 25 December.

In the 1500s, some Christians began worshipping God in new ways. One group, called the Puritans, were very serious. They did not like parties and merrymaking at Christmas. For a time, Puritans in Britain and North America stopped all the old Christmas customs.

However, after a few years, many Christians went back to their old ways of having fun at the Christmas festival.

▼ A Puritan leader stops games and drinking at Christmas.

Christmas Stories

There are many Christmas stories. They often tell about magical events or **miracles**.

The most famous Christmas story is about Santa Claus, or Father Christmas.

▶ Father Christmas wears a red coat and has a long white beard.

◀ To celebrate Saint Lucia's Day, girls in Sweden wear a white dress and a crown of candles.

The first story about Santa Claus comes from the Netherlands.

Santa Claus was really Saint Nicholas, a rich man who helped poor people. Nicholas was so kind that the Church made him a **saint**.

Today, people say that Santa Claus rides through the sky on a sledge pulled by reindeer. He stops at every house and leaves presents for the children.

▲ Saint Nicholas taking presents to children. In this picture he is helped by an angel.

Saint Lucia's Day

In Sweden, Saint Lucia's Day (13 December) comes just before Christmas. A story says that when Saint Lucia died, she was so good that she became a star in the sky.

◄ In northern Italy, children believe that a witch called Befana brings their presents.

Russians have a Christmas story about Baboushka (you say 'Ba-boosh-ka'). Baboushka gave some food to the wise men who were on their way to visit the baby Jesus. She wanted to go with them, but decided to finish her housework first.

The Miracle of the Poinsettia Plant

In Mexico, people tell a story about the red poinsettia plant. One Christmas, a little girl stood outside a church. She wanted to take a present into the church, but she was very poor and had no money.

An angel came, and told her to pick some weeds by the church door. Everybody laughed when she took the weeds into church, but suddenly a miracle happened. The leaves turned a beautiful red colour.

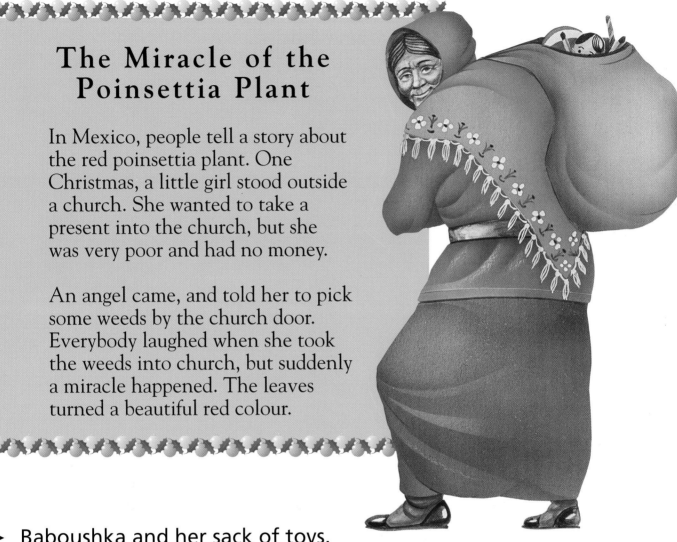

▶ Baboushka and her sack of toys.

The wise men could not wait so they went without Baboushka. She tried to follow, but she got lost. When she arrived in Bethlehem, Joseph, Mary and Jesus had already left.

Since then, Baboushka has travelled around the world looking for Jesus. At Christmas, she leaves a present at every house for every child, just in case they are the baby Jesus.

Customs

Giving presents is a popular custom at Christmas. In the **Bible**, the wise men took presents to the baby Jesus. Giving a present is a way of showing somebody that you care about them.

► Some children visit Santa Claus before Christmas. They tell him what presents they would like.

In many countries, children hang up long socks on Christmas Eve (24 December). They hope that Santa Claus will visit during the night. If they have been good during the past year, Santa will put presents in the socks.

In Germany, children find their presents left under the Christmas tree.

Other children have presents before Christmas, on 6 December. This is Saint Nicholas' Day.

When they go to bed on 5 December, Dutch children leave their **clogs** or shoes by the fireplace. They hope that Saint Nicholas will come down the chimney during the night and fill their shoes with gifts.

▲ Stockings filled with Christmas presents.

▲ A Korean family opening Christmas presents.

Piñatas

In Mexico, children get little presents from clay jars, hung in the trees. Children hit the jars with sticks to get the presents out. This game is called piñatas.

◄ This church service is in Bethlehem, the town where Jesus was born.

Nativity plays tell the story of how Jesus was born. People have been acting in nativity plays for hundreds of years.

◄ In Germany, boys dress up as the wise men. They carry a big star and walk through the streets singing carols.

◄ Children often act in nativity plays at church or school.

Special church services are important for Christians. Many people go to **midnight mass**, a service held at midnight on 24 December.

In Greece and Russia, the **Orthodox Church** has its main Christmas service on 6 January.

Good King Wenceslas

'Good King Wenceslas' is a famous Christmas carol. It tells the story of a king who lived a thousand years ago. On the day after Christmas, the feast of Saint Stephen, the king gave food and shelter to a poor man.

Shared Food

Sharing special meals with friends and family is an important part of Christmas.

In many countries, families have a special lunch on Christmas Day. They eat roast turkey, goose or duck.

In Britain, Christmas pudding is a popular way to end the meal. The pudding is made from dried fruit.

Sacred Bread

In Latvia, bread represents the body of Jesus, so it is very sacred, or holy.

Latvian children know that if they drop a piece of bread on the floor, they must pick it up and kiss it to say sorry.

◄ British people often have roast turkey for their Christmas lunch.

In Victorian times people added a sixpenny coin to the Christmas pudding mix. Finding the coin in your pudding was meant to bring good luck.

In Poland, people eat a Christmas meal on Christmas Eve. They begin eating when the first star comes out in the sky.

▼ A Russian family celebrates Christmas with fizzy wine.

Mince pies are popular in many countries. Hundreds of years ago, these pies were made out of minced meat. The meat was not very fresh, so cooks put many spices in the mixture to hide the bad taste. Today, the mincemeat in mince pies is really dried fruit.

◀ People in Italy make these special cakes at Christmas.

In the Netherlands, children make a cake called a *Letterbanket*. Cakes are made in the shape a letter from the alphabet. Each person in the family has the first letter of their name.

In Norway, children bake biscuits called 'thaw biscuits'. When the biscuits are cooked, the heat from the oven is supposed to melt the snow.

The southern part of the world has summer when the north has winter. This means that in countries like Australia, New Zealand and South Africa, Christmas is in the middle of summer.

When it is very hot, nobody wants to stay indoors, so Christmas dinner is often an outdoor meal.

Some families have a barbecue in their garden. Other people go to the beach and take a picnic.

A Christmas Feast in the Middle Ages

In the Middle Ages, rich people had a huge Christmas dinner. It lasted all day.

They ate many foods that we do not have today. One strange dish was the head of a boar, or wild pig. People also ate swans, and even peacocks.

◄ Christmas dinner in the garden in Australia.

Decorations

Many people decorate their homes and churches at Christmas. The oldest kinds of decoration are branches and leaves from **evergreen trees**.

▲ This painting shows the crown of thorns being placed on Jesus' head.

Long ago, people noticed that many trees lost their leaves in winter. They believed that the trees which kept their leaves had a special, magic power.

Holly trees and fir trees both have green leaves all year round.

Holly is important to Christians, because it reminds them of the death of Jesus. When Jesus was **crucified**, a crown made out of thorns was put on his head. The holly that people use to decorate their houses at Christmas represents the crown of thorns. The berries represent drops of blood.

Even before Jesus was born, people decorated their homes with evergreen branches in winter. The Romans put up ivy leaves and laurel leaves at the festival of Saturnalia.

Mistletoe

Mistletoe is a Christmas plant. Before Christians came to Britain, there were priests called druids, who believed the oak tree was very special. Mistletoe often grows on oak trees. The druids thought that the mistletoe plant kept the the tree alive during the winter. Today, people often hang mistletoe in their homes. If you stand under the mistletoe with somebody you like, you are supposed to give them a kiss.

◀ This Christmas decoration, with mistletoe, is called kissing bough.

◀ A church decorated with poinsettia plants and fir trees.

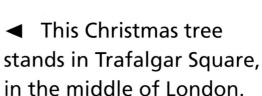

◄ This Christmas tree stands in Trafalgar Square, in the middle of London.

For hundreds of years, people in Germany have used fir trees for a Christmas decoration. About 150 years ago, this custom spread to other countries, including Britain and the USA.

◄ Life-sized models of Mary, Joseph and the baby Jesus outside a church in the USA. Can you see the shepherds and an angel?

◄ A woman in Moscow, Russia, lights a Christmas candle in a church.

Candles are an important part of many Christmas decorations. Nowadays, people also use electric lights.

Lights and candles remind Christians of a line in the Bible. It says that the baby Jesus was the 'light of the world'.

For Christians, the light from a candle has a special meaning. It gives a message of Christian hope – that the world can become a better place.

The Christian Calendar

Advent *December*
Advent begins on 1 December and lasts until Christmas. During Advent, Christians have special services, to get ready for Christmas.

Christmas Day
For most Christians, 25 December
The festival to celebrate the birthday of Jesus.

Epiphany *6 January*
The festival when Christians remember the three wise men. They came from the East to worship the baby Jesus.

► At Epiphany in Goa, India, children dressed as wise men ride to church on donkeys.

Shrove Tuesday *February*
The day before Lent begins. In many countries, this is a holiday, when people have parties and carnivals. In Britain it is also known as Pancake Day.

Lent *February/March/April*
Lent takes place during the six weeks before Easter. This is a serious time in the Christian religion, when Christians feel sorry for any wrong things they have done. Some people give up something they enjoy during Lent.

▼ Good Friday *March or April*

The day Christians remember that Jesus died on the cross.

Easter Sunday *March or April*

After Jesus was put to death, he came back to life again. Easter Sunday celebrates this event. It is the most important festival in the Christian year. The date of Easter Sunday changes from year to year.

Ascension Day *May or June*

After he came back to life, Jesus visited his followers. Then, on Ascension Day, he went up into heaven. Ascension Day is 40 days after Easter.

Pentecost *June*

On the day of Pentecost, the Holy Spirit came to earth. The Holy Spirit helps followers of Jesus to lead good lives, and do what Jesus wants them to do.

▼ Harvest Festival
September or October

Many churches have a festival in the autumn, to give thanks for the harvest. Churches are often decorated with food and flowers.

Glossary

Bible The Christian holy book. Part of the Bible tells the story of Jesus' life.

carols Special religious songs, sung at Christmas time.

clogs A type of wooden or wooden-soled shoe.

crucified Put to death by being fastened to a cross. This is how Jesus died.

evergreen trees Trees that have green leaves all year round.

midnight mass A church service. It takes place at midnight on Christmas Eve, so it is also the first service of Christmas Day.

miracle A miracle is an amazing event, something that does not normally happen.

Middle Ages The years from about AD 1000 to 1400.

nativity The nativity of Jesus was the time when he was born. A nativity play tells the story of how Jesus was born.

Orthodox Church A group of Christians. The Orthodox Church is the main kind of Christian religion followed in Greece and Russia.

Pope The Pope is the leader of a large group of Christians called Roman Catholics.

saint A very holy person, who behaves in a very good way.

Finding Out More

BOOKS TO READ

Celebration! by Barnabas and Anabel Kindersley
(Dorling Kindersley, 1997)

Christian Festivals by Saviour Pirotta
(Wayland, 2000)

Christmas by R. Thomson (Watts, 1994)

Long John Santa by Chris Powling
(Macdonald Young Books, 1999)

The Twelve Days of Christmas by Jan Brett
(Macdonald Young Books, 1999)

What Do We Know About Christianity?
by Carol Watson (Macdonald Young Books, 1997)

OTHER RESOURCE MATERIAL

Festivals Worksheets by Albany Bilbe and Liz
George (Wayland, 1998)

The Festival Shop stocks all kinds of educational
material relating to festivals. It also publishes
The Festival Year annually, a multifaith spiral
calendar of festivals.
The Festival Shop,
56 Poplar Road, Kings Heath, Birmingham B14 7AG
Tel: 0121 444 0444   Fax: 0121 441 5404

USEFUL ADDRESSES

To find out more about Christianity, you may find
these addresses useful:

The British Council of Churches,
2 Eaton Gate, London SW1W 9BT

Catholic Information Service,
74 Gallow Hill Lane, Abbotts Langley,
Hertfordshire WD5 OBZ

Christian Education Movement,
2 Chester House, Pages Lane,
London N10 1PR

Church of England Information Office,
Church House, Deans Yard,
London SW1P 3NZ

Committee for Extra-Diocesan Affairs,
Russian Orthodox Cathedral,
Ennismore Gardens, London SW7

The SHAP Working Party on World Religions,
c/o TheNational Society's RE Centre,
36 Causton Street, London SW1P 4AU
Tel: 0171 932 1194   Fax: 0171 932 1199

Society of Friends,
Friends House, Euston Road,
London NW1 2BJ

Index